C000303555

IMAGES OF
England

BELLINGHAM
NORTH TYNEDALE
AND REDESDALE

Tarset Station, *c.* 1900. The station was opened in 1862 and served the Border Counties railway line. It was the nearest station to the North Tyne village of Greenhaugh. Ladies, dressed in the style of the period, wait to board the train.

IMAGES OF
England

BELLINGHAM
NORTH TYNEDALE
AND REDESDALE

Compiled by
Ian Roberts and Moira West

TEMPUS

First published 1998
Reprinted 2004

Tempus Publishing Limited
The Mill, Brimscombe Port,
Stroud, Gloucestershire, GL5 2QG
www.tempus-publishing.com

© Ian Roberts and Moira West, 1998

The right of Ian Roberts and Moira West to be identified
as the Authors of this work has been asserted in accordance
with the Copyrights, Designs and Patents Act 1988.

All rights reserved. No part of this book may be reprinted
or reproduced or utilised in any form or by any electronic,
mechanical or other means, now known or hereafter invented,
including photocopying and recording, or in any information
storage or retrieval system, without the permission in writing
from the Publishers.

British Library Cataloguing in Publication Data.
A catalogue record for this book is available from the British Library.

ISBN 0 7524 1089 X

Typesetting and origination by Tempus Publishing Limited.
Printed in Great Britain by Midway Colour Print, Wiltshire

Kielder Castle, c. 1920. This view was taken before the castle and surrounding land had been
purchased and planted with trees by the Forestry Commission. The castle was built some 200
years before by the first Duke of Northumberland, who commissioned the architect William
Newton to design and build a shooting lodge. The original style was gothic. Parts of the castle
were redesigned by the fourth Duke during the nineteenth century and other alterations were
carried out by the eighth Duke in 1926. The castle is reputed to be haunted by the ghost of a
lady who walks the top floor of the main building.

Contents

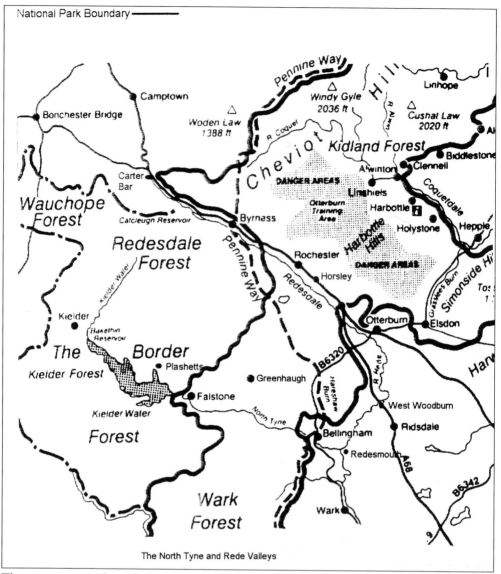

The North Tyne and Rede Valleys

The main centres of population in the North Tyne and Rede valleys.

Introduction

The photographs in this book depict life between 1890 and 1930 in the two upland regions of north-west Northumberland known as the North Tyne and Rede valleys. This is an area of outstanding natural beauty, comprising some 250,000 acres just south of the border with Scotland. North Tynedale is the valley hewn out by the North Tyne River, stretching from Wark to the Scottish border, while Redesdale is the valley formed by the River Rede and stretches from Redesmouth to the Carter Bar.

The population of this large area is small, as people are sparsely settled in villages, hamlets and outlying farms. In selecting these photographs, the authors have attempted to convey the changing shape of the landscape and the economic and social activities of the valleys during a critical period in the last century. The map on the opposite page shows the principal villages and geographical features mentioned in the pages which follow.

The historical background which has given to this landscape its hillforts, motte and bailey castles, peles, bastles and towers is turbulent and varied. Improvements in climate around 4000 BC made more permanent settlements of early nomadic farming folk possible in these northern valleys. Archaeological excavations of such sites as Tower Knowe, Belling Law and Kennel Hall Knowe in the North Tyne area attest to the fact that farming communities were still settled here during the pre-Roman period. The unearthing of pieces of coal, iron slag and stone moulds for casting metal, in addition to animal remains, provide evidence that there were early industrial as well as rural activities in this region.

The Roman conquest swept across northern Britain in 79-80 AD. The Romans recognised the value of Redesdale as a major communication route northwards and constructed through it a road into Scotland called Dere Street. They erected three outpost forts in Redesdale. The first was at West Woodburn where Dere Street crosses the river Rede, the second was sited at Blakehope near the second crossing of the river and the third fort was at High Rochester, guarding the approach to Redesdale from the north. The valley of North Tynedale was not included in this system of forts and roads.

The withdrawal of the Roman armies in the fifth century AD was followed by a sparsely documented period of conflict in which Anglo-Saxon invaders fought against the native British populations. In the sixth century the invaders had established the kingdoms of Bernicia and Deira which, by the seventh century, had merged to form the great kingdom of Northumbria, one of the major powers of Anglo-Saxon England. The upland areas of Northumbria were not suitable for arable farming of the type practised by the Anglo-Saxons. Evidence suggests that from the sixth to the mid-eleventh centuries these northern valleys were settled and defended by native British population groups.

From the early twelfth century Norman families began to acquire lands in Northumberland and castles were built at Wark and Bellingham. Both North Tynedale and Redesdale were 'Liberties' which meant that they were granted by the Crown to noblemen and had a different judicial status from the rest of England. The de Umfraville family held the Liberty of Redesdale from 1100 to the early fourteenth century and built as its headquarters the great motte and bailey castle at Elsdon. The Liberty of Tynedale, with its capital at Wark, was held at various periods by the Scottish kings. Dally Castle in Tynedale was built around 1237 by a Scottish nobleman.

The fourteenth to the seventeenth centuries saw prolonged periods of warfare between the English and the Scottish crowns in which shifting allegiances gave rise to cross-border reiving, lawlessness and great brutality. The people who remained in Redesdale and North Tynedale sought protection by allying themselves with one of the four major families (or 'graynes') in these valleys – the Charltons, Dodds, Milburns and Robsons. Economic prosperity on both sides of the border depended on the success of raiding forays in which cattle and booty from the other side were carried off.

After the abortive Jacobite rebellion of 1715 these northern valleys became more settled. During the seventeenth and eighteenth centuries, certain important landed families such as the Dukes of Northumberland carved out for themselves huge estates, which they then sub-divided and rented out as large sheep farms. The grazing in the valleys was of very poor quality so that in some places it took as much as three acres of land to support one sheep. In order to stock their farms successfully, tenant farmers developed a breed of sheep known as the Cheviot which was particularly suited to this rough terrain.

Gradually, as the population increased, small settlements such as Wark, Bellingham, Otterburn and others grew into larger and more integrated villages. Churches, schools and shops were built and the advent of the railways opened up the area to trading and commerce. At the same time, enterprising individuals began to exploit the natural mineral resources of the valleys. Coal mines were sunk, iron foundries were opened and quantities of building and road stone quarried from the hills. However, the practice of pastoral farming was still the mainstay of life in the valleys. In the nineteenth century, land agents were appointed to administer the business of the great estates and rented farms were traditionally passed from father to son.

Towards the end of the nineteenth century, pastoral agriculture in the Rede and North Tyne valleys became less profitable. Both landlords and tenants suffered considerable losses as a result of the falling prices of sheep and wool. Against this backdrop of agricultural recession the construction of the Catcleugh reservoir and the opening up of the military training area in Redesdale in the early twentieth century paved the way for certain irrevocable changes to both the economy and the topography of the valleys. After the First World War, sheep farming ceased to be a worthwhile proposition for landowners and thousands of acres of hill land were sold to the Forestry Commission. Vast tracts of trees were planted on what had previously been farmland. At the same time, the Army increased the size of its training area in Redesdale and families who had formerly been farmworkers now found employment as forestry workers or with the Army.

Finally, the upper part of the North Tyne valley was dammed in 1982 and the largest man-made lake in England, Kielder Water, was created from the inundation of thousands of acres to provide water for industrial Teesside. The topography of the landscape has now been fundamentally changed and, as a result, a new and successful tourist industry has begun to emerge.

This book preserves a pictorial record through which it is possible to gain an appreciation of a now vanished way of life in the North Tyne and Rede valleys.

Ian Roberts and Moira West,
Redesdale, Northumberland

One
Around Bellingham

Bellingham village taken from the Hesleyside Road before the Second World War. The two council estates, Westlands and Hillside, have not yet been built and there are no buildings on the right, between the bridge and the vicarage.

Dobbin's shop in 1919. Formerly a doctor's residence, it was taken over by Ted Dobbin, a photographer and newsagent, who lived above the shop. A placard outside Dobbin's announces the manifesto of the Miners' Federation, probably the 'Mines for the Nation' campaign of 1919. The premises on the right was Forster's (formerly Sutherland's) Temperance Hotel. The Boer War memorial on the left was first unveiled in this spot in 1904, but later moved to its more familiar location in Manchester Square.

Manchester Square and Town Hall, c. 1920. Situated on land formerly known as Muggers' Hill and donated by the Duke of Northumberland to the people of Bellingham, the Town Hall was built in 1862 at a cost of £600. The clock was donated by the old families of North Tynedale – the Charltons, Dodds, Robsons and Milburns. To the left of the Town Hall was Richard Pigg's general drapery and outfitters, now the Masonic Hall. The row of shops opposite the Town Hall included Coulson's saddlers and Hindmarsh's sweet shop.

UNVEILING OF THE DRINKING FOUNTAIN, BELLINGHAM

Unveiling the Boer War memorial and drinking fountain in June 1904. This now stands in Manchester Square but is shown here in its original location at the road junction near Lloyd's Bank. The memorial was the work of a Hexham sculptor, J. Milburn and paid for by subscriptions. Ulric Charlton of Hesleyside, who lived at Redesmouth Hall, had the honour of unveiling the memorial. It served the dual purpose of commemorating those villagers who died in the Boer War and also supplying the village with fresh drinking water. The soldier on the memorial wears the uniform of the Northumberland Fusiliers, whose First and Second Battalions fought the Boers. Note the gas lamp on top of the memorial, later replaced by an electric lamp and finally removed completely.

11

The Railway Hotel, *c.* 1930. Situated in the main street in Bellingham, this hotel is now called 'The Cheviot'. In the time of the Hareshaw Iron Works and before the advent of the railway, it is believed to have been a coaching inn called 'The Engine' and later 'The Furnace'. The hotel was privately owned and never belonged to the railway company. The premises to the right of the hotel, which is now a craft shop, was once owned by a watchmaker and later became a barber's shop.

The Tarset Road at the west end of Bellingham, around the time of the First World War. The entrance on the left led to the Reed's Trust Charity School, which is now the Reed Hall. The house on the right is 'Tyne View'. Until 1900 the only house between the Reed School and the bridge over the Tyne was the rectory, but the early twentieth century saw the development of housing to the west of the village. The iron railings, below the pillar to the right, mark the gardens of these new houses, built on what was formerly grazing land.

Percy Street, *c.* 1920. In 1838, when the Hareshaw Iron Works commenced operations, housing had to be provided for its workforce. Five rows of cottages were constructed on the area now occupied by the modern Hillside estate. One row, called Percy Street, had its exit on the Woodburn Road just above the end of the modern Percy Terrace. This row consisted of twenty houses. The living accommodation of each comprised a large living-room and pantry downstairs, with a sleeping loft above. The Iron Works closed in 1848 and by 1854 only nine of these houses were occupied, at a rent of a shilling per week. By 1897 all four other rows had been demolished.

Waverley House, *c.* 1920. Situated on the corner of Reedsmouth Road, this was first used as a dwelling house, later a shop, before reverting to a house. Note the railway bridge spanning the Woodburn Road in the background, which was built to the west of the railway station. The bridge was first opened in 1861 and removed soon after the line was closed in 1956.

Hareshaw Burn, *c.* 1920. This shows the lower end of the Hareshaw Burn before it enters the area formerly occupied by Hareshaw Iron Works. Signs of former excavation and remains of spoil heaps can be seen on the landscape. The house in the background was known as 'Old Len's House', after an itinerant agricultural labourer who once lived there. The house, which was demolished in 1995 when the golf course was extended, had been erected by the Iron Works and was probably occupied by the linesman who maintained the waggon way from the Hareshaw Colliery.

Ford and footbridge over Hareshaw Burn at Fallow Green, *c.* 1910. The ford has now been replaced by a load-bearing bridge. The building with the dovecote at the back was the village smithy at one time but is now a private dwelling. The stone cottages which can be seen below the church have been demolished and replaced by Sunnydale and Riverside Garage.

Bellingham after the thunderstorm and flood of 1911. The most spectacular flash flood for which we have visual evidence in Bellingham took place on the Hareshaw Burn on 14 May 1911 as a result of a localised thunderstorm. The burn rapidly rose more than fifteen feet above normal level, sweeping bridges away and leaving part of the village under water. The area shown is Fallow Green close to the Gasworks, where property was damaged and the footbridge washed away. The Gasworks was in operation from 1864 to 1938 and was situated by the burn in the area now occupied by the property called 'Meadow's Edge'.

Brookside Place after the thunderstorm of 1911. The most serious damage was confined to the area along the burn as shown here. Large sections of buildings were swept away by the flood which did not abate for two hours. Some buildings had to be demolished as a result.

Jubilee Day, May 1935. Many of the villages celebrated the Silver Jubilee of King George V's Coronation. In Bellingham this took the form of a procession by almost the entire population to the Riverdale Hall field for a picnic and sporting events. Some of the war veterans are shown here, wearing their medals.

Two

Around
North Tynedale

Wark, Greenhaugh, Plashetts, Falstone, Kielder

THE SQUARE, WARK.

Published by Messrs. Hunter, Hexham

The square in Wark, c. 1900. Wark was the capital of the regality of Tynedale in the Middle Ages and even had a castle of its own. The square or village green is an area of common land administered by the Parish Council where travellers are permitted to camp for twenty-four hours before moving on. Note that the centre of the square has a young chestnut tree, planted in 1887 to commemorate Queen Victoria's Golden Jubilee. The mature tree still stands on the square today.

The Black Bull and the Grey Bull Inns, before the First World War. At one time, Wark boasted five public houses of which three still remain. Two are shown here. The Black Bull was first licensed in 1831 and has been altered and enlarged a number of times. Next door is the Grey Bull, licensed in 1838, which advertised a well known brand of whisky on its end wall.

The Highland Drove Inn, 1913. The inn was known until shortly after 1825 as 'The Drove of Cattle'. Both names reflect the fact that this was a popular halting place for Scottish drovers on route with their cattle to the markets in the industrial towns south of the border. The popularity of inns such as this waned as railways replaced droving as a means of conveying cattle to market. In the year this photograph was taken, its license was withdrawn and it is now a private house.

Church Lane, Wark in 1910. A lane which is now much altered and is the main road from Wark to Bellingham. Northumberland House and beyond it Chapel House can be seen on the right. On the left of this lane, close to the village, stone built cottages were later erected and occupied by miners who worked in the Sutty Row Colliery not far from the village. Their homes were conveniently situated close to one of the village pumps which was located in the area in front of the present police house.

Wark village, 1920. Wark Town Hall, erected as the Mechanics' Institute for the village in 1873, can be seen in the background. The men are playing quoits, a traditional North country village game. The bearded gentleman to the left was one of Wark's most famous residents – Mr William Charlton. He held the tenancy of the Black Bull Inn but moved to farm at Battlesteads in 1889. In 1912 Mr Charlton brought a new water supply to the village from a deep cold spring at Latterford. It gave many Wark residents fresh piped water and remained the main water supply until 1956.

The village blacksmith, Nicholas Pattison. The smithy was situated next door to the Battlesteads Hotel on the Hexham Road. It is believed to have been built much earlier than Forge Cottage across the road, which was the blacksmith's house, built in 1904. The smithy, which was also a wheelwright's shop, continued in operation until 1964 when the advent of motor cars and the increasing use of tractors on farms forced its closure.

Wark Mart, c. 1920. The mart is believed to have been one of the earliest established in the area in the 1860s and was located on land now occupied by the doctor's surgery near the Battlesteads Hotel. The main sale was held on the Thursday closest to 11 September. In addition to the usual cattle and sheep trading, the mart was also an important venue for the sale of foals in the North of England. The village school was usually closed on mart day to enable village children to enjoy the funfair on the village square. Although it was also an important centre for sheep grading and sales during the Second World War, the mart was closed down in 1947.

Coal is a rich resource in the North Tyne valley. Commercial and private mines were plentiful in the nineteenth and early twentieth centuries. William Charlton of Battlesteads also owned the Sutty Row Colliery near Birtley which gave employment to a number of men from Wark village. The staff of the colliery in 1945 can be seen above. Standing, left to right: David White, Jack Meikle and John Reed. Seated, left to right: Andrew Haldane, Walter Hall, Ralph Liddle, Cyril Cooper and Joe Bell.

Also shown here is a weekly pay slip for Cyril Cooper in 1944. Note that although Cyril was in receipt of a tax refund that week, he still had to pay for his own insurance and for the carbide used in his lamp when working underground. His daily pay then was eleven shillings and eight pence – the equivalent of 58 pence today!

Charlton Collieries, Ltd.

SUTTY ROW COLLIERY.

No. _20_   Pay 194_4_

Bargain Shifts.

Note No. _12_

Datal Shifts.

Name _C Cooper_

	£	s.	d.	£	s.	d.
Piece Work Earnings ...						
6 d 11/8	3	10	0			
Tax Refund	1	3	0			
OFFTAKES:—				4	13	0
	4	13	0			
Explosives						
Insurance 1 9						
Corbuda 6						
2/3					2	3
Balance ...				4	10	9

21

Philipson's shop in Wark village before the First World War. There were fourteen shops in the village in the early twentieth century, which had been reduced to eleven by 1939. Many of these have now closed and been turned into private houses. Philipson's was one of the larger shops, selling not only a wide range of groceries but also linoleum and other floor coverings. In the background, on the right, can be seen the shop's flour and bacon warehouse from which deliveries were made to a wide range of farms in the locality. Philipson's is now known as Walton's, the butchers shop.

Park End, c. 1908. The greater part of Wark village was at one time owned by the Ridley family who came to the area in the late seventeenth century and lived at Park End mansion shown here. The front of the house faces east overlooking the North Tyne river, and has two additional wings, completed around 1830.

Greenhaugh village, *c.* 1920. It consisted of dwellings occupied mainly by farmworkers who worked at the two large houses nearby, Greenhaugh Hall and Sidwood. This view of the village is taken from the rear entrance to Greenhaugh Hall, built by the Spencer family who owned Spencer's Iron Works on the River Tyne at Newburn. On the right is the cottage tenanted by the gardener to the hall. The village post office was located in the last house on the right.

A close-up of Greenhaugh post office in 1924. Like many rural post offices of the period it was located in a private house. It was run by Mrs Margaret Thompson. It is now no longer used for this purpose.

The Old Drift at Seldom Seen, Plashetts, c. 1900. Coal resources at Plashetts are documented from the 1850s when they were mined for use at Kielder Castle. The first colliery and settlement opened by the Plashetts' Coal and Coke Company was known as Seldom Seen because of the remoteness of its location high up in the Belling Burn valley. A row of two storey cottages was built to house mining families and a rail link to the main line was constructed. On 24 June 1862 the railway to Plashetts was opened and the coal company began to send coal away for sale. At the time this photograph was taken, the mine had been closed and these houses were being used by miners working in other pits in the Plashetts area.

Shop Row, Plashetts, c. 1900. In the second settlement at Plashetts, the street built on either side of the waggon way was known as Shop Row because the last two houses had been converted into the company shop. The waggon way was the only form of access for goods to the village and a delivery of food and other supplies is being made into the shop in this photograph. These horse-drawn waggons also carried coal to the processing plant where it was then placed in larger trucks and transported on the main railway.

Plashetts village, c. 1900. A broader view of the village shows the Methodist chapel on the far left, built in 1874 on land donated by the Duke of Northumberland. Many miners were Methodists, a faith particularly strong in mining areas in England and Wales. There was no resident minister and the church was served by the minister from Bellingham. Just beyond the allotments to the right is the village school. Opened in 1891, the school could at first only accommodate 64 pupils. As the new company which had taken control of the mines in the late 1880s expanded the colliery, the school-age population also grew and the school was extended to take 90 pupils with two teachers.

Stable Row, Plashetts, c. 1900. This row of brick built cottages was constructed near the stables for the pit ponies at the time the mines were expanded in the 1880s. The large number of children shown here indicate why it was necessary to expand the size of the village school in the 1890s.

St Peter's church, Falstone, *c.* 1925. As is the case with many of the North Tyne parishes, Falstone owes its origins to the breaking up of the huge Simonburn parish. First built in 1824, it was designed by Newcastle architects John and Benjamin Green. The style adopted here was similar to that of Wark and Thorneyburn. The church is shown here against the backdrop of Yarrow Moor, long before the advent of tree plantations or the Kielder Dam.

Smale Farm near Falstone, before the First World War. This farm, which was over two thousand acres in size, was leased from the Duke of Northumberland at this time by the Murrays, a father and son partnership. However, they found the land extremely difficult to farm. It was then leased by the Duke to the Forestry Commission in 1925 on an experimental tree-farming lease, making it the first part of the huge Kielder Forest.

The Kielder Dam under construction, 1975-81. During the 1960s pressure grew for a large water source to supply not only Tyneside but also industrial Teesside. This resulted in a scheme to dam the North Tyne at Kielder which would provide a solution to any future water shortage. The complete project, which was opened in 1982, cost £167 million, considerably more than the original estimate of £23 million.

Kielder Station, c. 1920. When first opened, the station signboard said 'Kieldar' but this was changed to 'Kielder Forest' in the 1940s. The signal box was added to the simple platform layout in 1895. Further changes were made in 1925 to enable the Forestry Commission to carry timber out of Kielder. The line was closed in 1956. The two cottages have since been converted into a private dwelling and a petrol station. The signal box has been demolished.

Kielder Viaduct in 1925. This viaduct was designed by Nicholson and Tone, engineers for the Border Counties railway, to span the Tyne at Kielder. Built by William Hutchinson, it was opened in 1862 and, being 392 feet long and 55 feet high, is one of the most impressive examples of Victorian industrial architecture in Northumberland. The viaduct became the property of the Forestry Commission with the closure of the railway line in 1956. It was sold in the 1960s to the Newcastle Society who had it approved as a listed structure, thus guaranteeing its preservation. Kielder School, which was closed in 1963 and is now under the waters of the reservoir, can be seen on the left.

Three
Around Redesdale

Redesmouth, East Woodburn,
West Woodburn, Ridsdale, Otterburn, Horsley,
Rochester, Byrness, Catcleugh, Elsdon

Redesmouth Station, *c.* 1926. The Border Counties railway line went through the North Tyne valley, while the Wansbeck line from Morpeth over the Wanney hills to West Woodburn served the Rede valley. Both lines intersected at Redesmouth (or Reedsmouth) Junction. The station was first opened in 1862 as a wayside halt, but became much larger with the arrival of the Wansbeck line in 1865. The station and the lines were closed in the 1960s.

Redesmouth Hall in the 1920s. The hall was owned by the Haggerston family which was one of the oldest Catholic families in Northumberland. It is of a predominantly nineteenth century design, but incorporates architectural features from the two previous centuries. At the time that this photograph was taken, the hall was rented from Sir Carnaby Haggerston by Mr Ulric Charlton, whose car, one of the earliest in the district, is seen in the drive.

Redesmouth Mill, *c.* 1920. Corn was grown on farms in the area, including those on the Haggerston estate. Using the abundant local water supply, the Haggerstons constructed this mill for the use of their tenants only a short distance from Redesmouth Hall. When milling operations ceased, the mill was converted into a small farm.

East Woodburn, c. 1920. This was the main village on the drove road from Scotland, which can be seen going uphill in the background. The loading bay for the Darney Quarry, where many of the villagers worked, is visible next to the drove road. The tramway from the quarry to the loading bay can also be seen here.

The Queen's Head Inn in East Woodburn, c. 1900. This inn was in the centre of the village. The landlord at this time, Andrew Ridley, can be seen outside the inn with members of his family. It is now a private house.

Harewalls Farm, c. 1920. This shows a celebration hosted by the Hall family at the farm they tenanted near East Woodburn. A typical upland sheep farm, it was situated a short way up the Lisles Burn. Parties of the size shown were rare and usually only took place to mark weddings or the completion of the hay harvest. The wedding of Miss Lily Hall to Mr G. Craghill is depicted here.

The Bay Horse Inn in West Woodburn, c. 1920. The area around the inn is the oldest part of the village. In 1832 there were only about ten houses in West Woodburn, together with a mill and the inn. It can be dated from the lintel above the door on which 1797 is carved. An advertisement about the inn at the time of the photograph describes its cosy and restful rooms and a kitchen providing meals using locally grown farm produce.

West Woodburn Station, c. 1925. This view of the station is taken from the site of Parkhead Quarry. The large building to the rear of the signal box was Matthew Graham's store and warehouse, used to supply the village and also Graham's other shops in Ridsdale and Rochester. The large house, to the left beyond the station, is Alma House, the former residence of William Pigg who had operated Parkhead Quarry before its closure.

The village hall in West Woodburn in 1907. Villagers had opened a highly popular subscription library and reading room in December 1883 and pressure for a building in which to hold communal meetings resulted in the construction of the village hall or institute as it was sometimes called. The hall was used for village functions, whist drives and other activities and still exists today. The stile on the left led to the footpath to East Woodburn.

Hillcrest, West Woodburn in 1935. Taken from the north end of the village, this shows the A68 road winding down the hill over the bridge. On the immediate left, at the top of the hill, are the houses built as modern housing for rent by Bellingham Rural District Council. The next building down the hill is the Methodist chapel, built in 1866, which has now fallen into disuse. The later Whiteacre council houses, behind the chapel, were not built until after the Second World War.

Foundry Cottages at Ridsdale, c. 1920. Ridsdale was built in the 1840s to house the workforce employed in the iron foundry, established to exploit the local deposits of coal and iron ore. The foundry itself was located just to the left of the houses shown here, which were all part of the foundry yard complex around the blast furnaces. It is still possible to see the substantial remains of the engine house and the humps and hollows where the coke furnaces were located. In the distance can be seen Sarelaw Cottages where Matthew Graham had his store.

St George's Square, Ridsdale, *c.* 1920. This view is taken from behind the village pump, looking westwards. The square was built by Sir William Armstrong around 1865 during the second phase of Ridsdale's involvement in iron-mining. The village inn, the large building with the signboard above the door, was also built in the Armstrong era. At that time it was called 'The Armstrong Arms' and run by the Nesbit family who were also the village butchers. It is now known as 'The Gun'.

Ridsdale Shop and pump, *c.* 1920. Despite the fact that this second mining operation closed down in 1879, the village continued to house colliery workers, railway employees and farm workers. This shop, run by the Slassor family from the late nineteenth century until the 1990s, was an important feature of village life. To the right of the shop was the village pump, or 'pant' as the villagers called it, which supplied fresh water to the village until a supply was piped from Catcleugh in the 1950s.

Otterburn village, *c.* 1900. The white building on the left is the village inn, first known as the Percy Arms but at this time called the Murray Arms, after the owners of the estate of which it formed a part. The inn was an important halting place for stage coaches on the journey from Edinburgh to London. The post was collected from here before the railway was built. The inn is now known again as the Percy Arms. The church and spire of St John's Anglican church, built in 1857, can be seen in the far distance.

The east side of Otterburn village, *c.* 1900. The village store is located in the centre of the row of houses opposite the inn. At the far end of the road, shrouded by the tree, was the rectory used by the Anglican vicars of Otterburn until the late 1980s, when it was replaced by a modern rectory built beside the church.

Clearing up after the flood of 1907. Otterburn had experienced several floods and some, like those of 1792, 1818 and 1839, had caused serious damage in the village. A severe, localised thunderstorm on 9 June 1907 caused the Otter Burn to rise very rapidly and inundate the village with flood water which measured five feet at its deepest. The inn, sited close by the bridge, was flooded and a huge amount of debris carried into its forecourt.

The old bridge at Otterburn after the 1907 flood. The force of the flood waters and the debris carried downstream by the Otter Burn caused the arch of the bridge to clog up and tore away its southern end as shown here. It could not be repaired and the County Council constructed a new bridge, higher, wider and more ornate than its predecessor.

Foster's Garage at Otterburn, *c.* 1917. The first garage in Redesdale was opened in Otterburn by Joseph Foster on the eve of the First World War. This view clearly shows the motor cars, motor bikes and bicycles which the proud proprietor, seen here standing on the left, could hire out or repair.

"FOSTER'S"

 OSTER'S is the Garage at Otterburn where you can Buy Motors, Cycles, &c., and Accessories, and where you can have your Car Repaired as though it were fresh from the Factory. But it is more than a Country Garage. Foster's is a Reedwater institution and a Public Necessity. When you wish to explore the district Foster's Car will meet you at Woodburn Station, or any other Station, and take you on your way rejoicing. And when you decide to make your home up here, it is Foster's Motor Truck that will bring your household goods along the winding Watling Street. When you have transportation troubles, Foster's will fix you. And when you take into your head to buy a car, Foster's advice will save you good money. He is familiar with practically every make of Car, and knows most of them intimately. :: ::

JOSEPH FOSTER,
The Garage,
OTTERBURN.
Telephone: No. 7, Otterburn.

The *Reedwetter Review*, a local magazine produced by Charles Pigg of West Woodburn in 1917, advertised Foster's garage.

Otterburn Hall, c. 1910. The hall was constructed during the late nineteenth century by the brother of the fifth Duke of Atholl, Lord James Murray, who had purchased Otterburn estate in 1870. Bricks made from clay on the nearby estate were used in its construction. Lord James died in 1874 at the age of 54 but his widow remained at the hall until her death in 1888. Since there was no male heir to inherit the hall it passed to their youngest surviving daughter Caroline who never married. She continued to live there and managed the estate until she sold the property to the Morrison-Bell family and moved away from the area. The hall is now used as a holiday and conference centre.

Elsdon Church and Green, *c.* 1890. An elderly resident of the village stands on the village green in front of the parish church dedicated to St Cuthbert. Parts of this church can be dated back to the twelfth century. It was rebuilt in the fourteenth century and restored in 1837 and again in 1877. It has a fine collection of carved gravestones in the churchyard, dating back to the eighteenth century. Behind the church can be seen the roof of Elsdon Tower, constructed in the fifteenth century and later the home of the Anglican minister.

Elsdon Mote Hills, *c.* 1900. The Hills, dug out of a glacial drift, were the site of an early castle of the Lords of Redesdale and the centre of civil government in the early Middle Ages. The mound on the left was the site of a wooden tower which had in front a rectangular bailey surrounded by a large earth bank with an outer ditch. This stronghold was in an ideal position to dominate the crossing of the Elsdon Burn and the village. The castle fell into disuse when the Lords of Redesdale built a stone castle at Harbottle some miles to the east and took up residence there.

The first car at Elsdon, *c.* 1910. This photograph combines the arrival of the first car in the village with the ancient custom of riding the bounds, which took place during the August Fair in Elsdon. The riders are about to depart on their journey, after which they all gathered on the green for the proclaiming of the fair in mime.

Elsdon Water Mill, *c.* 1910. Elsdon village was surrounded by a large common on which the cattle and sheep of the local farmers were pastured. In 1731 this common was enclosed and grain was grown on the flat, well-drained land close to the rivers and streams. This water mill was constructed in the first half of the eighteenth century. The Hall family operated it from around 1760 until 1938 when it closed down – the last water mill to cease operation in the Rede valley.

The Redesdale Arms Hotel at Horsley, *c.* 1930. This hotel is situated in the hamlet lying between Otterburn and Rochester and was known for many years as the Horsley Inn. The tenant and licensee at this time was Ben Prior. The inn, also known as 'The First and Last in England' depending on whether it was approached from the Scottish side or the English side of the border, had a distinguished history as a halting place for stage coaches. The hotel is named from the title of Redesdale borne by the Mitford family, part of whose estate it has been since the end of the eighteenth century.

The vicarage at Horsley, *c.* 1910. This building is situated at the back of Holy Trinity church, Horsley, between the Redesdale Arms and the village of Rochester. The church was built by Lord Redesdale in 1844 for the use of the local people living on his estate. Initially looked after by a curate from Elsdon parish, Horsley church became a parish in its own right in 1884 and the vicarage was constructed at this time. The first vicar at Horsley, the Revd Thomas Stephens, is seen here rolling the tennis court. The church, with its memorials to the Mitford family, may be visited but the vicarage has been in private ownership since the 1960s.

Rochester village, c. 1910. This early view shows one of the main blocks of houses in the central part of Rochester village. Almost all the houses in this village belonged to the Redesdale estate. They had recently been renovated and provided with piped running water from a private supply on the estate in 1900. This was in contrast to the village of Ridsdale which depended on the village pump for another fifty years thereafter.

Rochester village and army camp, c. 1925. A more extensive view of the village, it extended from the post office on the right down to Graham's shop. Most of the houses had substantial well-tended gardens on the opposite side of the road. In the background to the left, the army camp can be seen. Soldiers were sent to Redesdale for training and accommodated in tents such as these. The more permanent army buildings were used as stables for horses. The building on the extreme left in the background is Birdhopecraig Hall which had been sold to the army by Lord Redesdale and was used at this time as the officers' mess. It was destroyed by fire in 1957.

Part of High Rochester, c. 1910. Located above the village of Rochester, this hamlet is situated entirely within the walls of a Roman fort. The houses shown run along the inside of the north wall of the fort, much of which was recycled for use in the houses' walls. The single storey cottages on the right have now been demolished. One of the houses, Rose Cottage, contains the remains of a bastle house, a sixteenth century fortified dwelling, in its walls.

Birdhopecraig Lodge, c. 1910. One of the early cars is shown outside the lodge attached to Birdhopecraig Hall, north of Rochester. The hall and the lodge at its entrance were built by Lord Redesdale as a shooting box for the estate in the first half of the nineteenth century. In 1911, the hall, lodge and more than 2,700 acres of surrounding farm land was sold to the War Office for use as an army artillery training area. The hall was accidentally burnt down in 1957 and the lodge is all that now remains.

Pity Me Farm on the Bellshield Burn, *c.* 1914. This was a sheep farm of 645 acres on the Redesdale estate. The name is popularly thought to have originated in describing the lonely fate of those forced to live on this isolated farm. This house was usually occupied by a shepherd and his family, and a byre was also provided for his cow. Pity Me was part of the land sold to the army in 1911 to form the new training area.

Byrness church and farm, *c.* 1890. The church was built in 1796 and dedicated to St Francis of Assisi. Byrness farmhouse can be seen on the opposite side of the road. The farm was the most northerly property on the Redesdale estate. At this time it was tenanted by Jacob Robson, who rented over 6,000 acres. Robson was considered an authority on Cheviot sheep and also ran the Border Hunt.

Catcleugh Farm and Reservoir, *c.* 1950. The reservoir, which had then been in existence for some fifty years, can be seen in the background. The farm belonged to the Duke of Northumberland but was sold in the 1930s to become part of the Forestry Commission's Redesdale Forest. The land where the sheep are grazing is now a forest plantation and the present farm consists of a small number of fields with the house and buildings.

Carter Bar in 1937. There were considerable snowfalls in the winter of 1937 and the main road to Scotland over Carter Bar had to be kept open if possible. In the absence of more modern snow ploughs, clearing the snow was usually accomplished by a small army of workmen with shovels, as shown here.

Four

The Working Day

*Farming, Marts and Shows, Mills and Weaving,
Coalmining, Quarrying and Roadmaking,
Iron Founding, The Dams, Inns and Shops*

West Kielder Farm in the 1920s. This farm was just over 8,000 acres and belonged to the Duke of Northumberland. It was divided into three parts: West Kielder (or Raven's Hill), Scaup and Kielder Head. This view shows the Raven's Hill house and farm buildings just above Kielder village. In 1921, as a result of a fall in rents, the farm was split in two. However, even this failed to make a profit and most of the land was then sold to the Forestry Commission.

William Hodgson (1846-1907), land agent for Redesdale. One of the most important men in the Rede valley, Hodgson came at the age of thirteen to live with his uncle, Edward Lawson, then land agent for Lord Redesdale. Hodgson assisted his uncle for twenty years and succeeded him as agent when the latter died in 1878. He lived at Redesdale Cottage near the Redesdale Arms Hotel and from there traversed the valley to supervise the estate farms and cottages.

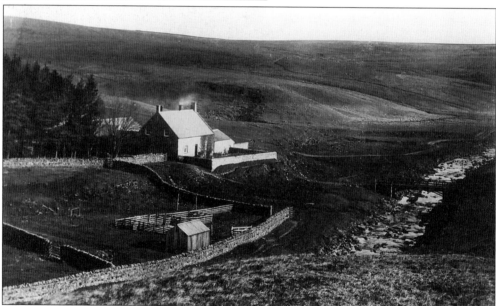

Cranecleugh Farm in 1935. A large farm in North Tynedale, which, together with the neighbouring Bull Crag Farm, was owned by the Duke of Northumberland. Together, both farms measured nearly 7,000 acres in extent but had very poor grazing and could only carry one adult sheep to every three acres. The farm was sold to the Forestry Commission in 1936 and planted with trees in part. Other parts of the farm are now under Kielder Reservoir.

Clipping day at Cranecleugh in 1912. The farm carried a flock of two thousand sheep and a herd of twenty cows. In 1912 the farm was leased from the Duke by William Pickering who ran it with the help of three shepherds and their families. An important day in the farmer's calendar was clipping day when all hands came to help. The sheep shown here are Scottish Blackface. The man second from the left is gripping the sheep's horn with his left hand before starting to clip with his right.

Clipping sheep in 1924. This operation was traditionally carried out using hand clippers in late June in the North Tyne and Rede valleys. The sheep has just been shorn here and the fleece put to one side ready for rolling and packing. The man on the right is marking the sheep with the owner's mark before it is returned to the flock. Marking, or buisting, was done with a metal rod at the end of which the owner's initials or another distinctive symbol was mounted in metal. The rod was dipped in tar and the sheep branded.

Clipping sheep, *c.* 1900. Taken on an unidentified farm in the Rede valley, this photograph shows that clipping day was an annual event in which the shepherds' wives also played their part. The lady at the end of the table is helping roll fleeces ready for packing. The fleece was laid on the table, clean side down, then rolled from the fore end towards the tail. The tail wool was twisted into a rough rope and used to bind the fleece into a roll.

The washing pool at Yearhaugh, *c.* 1900. North of the old bridge over the Rede near East Woodburn is a very deep pool favoured for washing sheep. It was possible to drive them to the very edge of the riverbank and then ease them straight into deep water. The stony bottom of the pool and the shingle bank on the opposite side meant that the sheep did not become muddy in the process. Sheep were washed eight to ten days before clipping to ensure the fleeces were clean and dry.

Driving sheep to Bellingham Mart, *c.* 1920. In 1861 the Duke of Northumberland was petitioned by the people of Bellingham to allow sales of wool and sheep to take place three times a year in the village. As a result, a mart was opened in 1862 close to the railway along the Otterburn road. Some stock was brought by train but the vast majority, like the Cheviot sheep shown here, were driven by shepherds and their dogs along the road.

Bellingham Mart, *c.* 1930. Farmers congregated outside the mart to discuss the day's events and study catalogues before selling began. As the pressure of trade and the amount of stock increased in the locality the sales became more frequent. A covered ring was built in which the stock could be shown and sold more comfortably.

THE ANNUAL
NORTH TYNE & REDESDALE
CHEVIOT SHEEP SHOW,

WILL BE HELD

At FALSTANE,

On Wednesday, 12th September next,

WHEN PREMIUMS WILL BE OFFERED AS BELOW:---

Class First.

For the BEST SINGLE TUP, not less than Two Years Old, bred or bought by the Competitor, to have served Ewes in the District, or to serve in the District the ensuing season, - - - - - -
For the SECOND BEST   Do.   Do. - - - - -
For the THIRD BEST   Do.   Do. - - - - -

Class Second.

For the BEST PEN of Three Two Years Old Tups, bred in the District, -
For the SECOND BEST   Do.   Do. - - - -

Class Third.

For the BEST PEN of Three One-year-old Tups, bred in the District, -
For the SECOND BEST   Do.   Do. -

Class Fourth.

For the BEST PEN of Four Tup Lambs, bred in the District, -
For the Second Best   Do.   Do. - - -

Class Fifth.

For the BEST PEN of Five Ewes, bred in the District from the regular Hirsel, to have reared Lambs this Season,
For the SECOND BEST   Do.   Do. - - - -

Class Sixth.

For the BEST PEN of Five Two-year-old Ewes, bred in the District from the regular Hirsel, - - - -
For the SECOND BEST   Do.   Do. -

Class Seventh.

For the BEST PEN of Five Gimmers, bred in the District from the regular Hirsel, -
For the SECOND BEST   Do.   Do. - -

Class Eighth.

For the BEST PEN of Five Ewe Lambs, bred by the Competitor, and to have been summered the same as the regular Hirsel - - -
For the Second Best   Do.   Do.— -

£2 to be added to the Shearlings by Sir M. W. RIDLEY, Bart.

£3 will be given for the First, Second, Third, and Fourth Best Single Ewe, bred in the District from the Regular Hirsel, the Property of Subscribers' Shepherds.

The Judges will decide any Sweepstakes entered into by Individuals.—Intending Competiters must give notice to Mr J. ROBSON of East Kielder, or to Mr N. R. REED of Birness, on or before Friday the 7th September next.

☞ The Stock to be Penned by Ten o'Clock on the Morning of the Show.

DINNER ON THE TABLE AT HALF-PAST THREE O'CLOCK.

Tickets, Five Shillings each, to be had of the Innkeeper at Falstane.

N.B.—TUPS WILL ALSO BE SHOWN FOR SALE.

FALSTANE, 19th August, 1849.

W. Easton, Printer, Jedburgh.

This advertisement publicised the Falstone Show of 1849.

Falstone Show, *c.* 1911. Agricultural societies became very popular in Victorian times and most had an annual show. Pens of Cheviot sheep are seen here. The bearded gentleman on the right is John Robson of the Newton Farm at Tarset, one of the most important breeders of Cheviot sheep at that time. John won awards at local shows, at the Border Union Show and at the internationally famous Highland and Agricultural Show. He was also the first secretary of the Cheviot Sheep Society, a post he filled with distinction for over thirty years.

The Dodds at Catcleugh in 1951. Catcleugh Farm was nearly 6,000 acres in extent, making it one of the largest in the Rede valley. In 1951 the Dodd family, tenants for well over a century, gave up their tenancy. This photograph, taken just before the sale of the farm stock, shows Mrs Laura Dodd talking to two members of the Roberton family who had ridden over from their farm in Scotland. Mrs Dodd's relative, Jacob Robson (Young Jake), Master of the Border Foxhounds who farmed at Coldtown near West Woodburn, is also in the group.

Stacking hay at Foundry Farm, Bellingham in 1913. This photograph was taken during haymaking, a busy time on upland farms. Grass was cut and turned until it was dry enough to be gathered together into small stacks called pikes. The pike was placed on a small flat cart, called a bogey, which was harnessed to a horse. The pike was led to thefarmyard where it was added to the large hayrick which would be thatched and made weatherproof for winter. Three such bogeys are shown in front of the Foundry Farm hayrick, sited where the blast furnaces once stood.

Hill drainage at Catcleugh Farm in 1908. The tenants of all the upland sheep farms in the North Tyne and Rede valleys were obliged by agreement with the landlords to keep open the ditches which drained the rough fell pastures. These drains were V-shaped ditches over half a metre deep which carried surface water away to the streams. In this way sheep diseases like liver fluke and foot rot were kept at bay. A gang employed to open the drains at Catcleugh Farm is shown here. Note the heart-shaped spade carried by the third man from the right which was used to cut the ditches. The others carry hooked forks and lighter spades to clear away the turf and complete the drain.

Power loom weaving at Otterburn Mill, *c.* 1910. A mill for spinning and weaving wool has been in existence at Otterburn since the eighteenth century. Most of the wool was bought from local farmers who were sometimes paid in woollen goods woven from their wool. A power loom used to weave large quantities of cloth is shown here. In 1821 this mill was taken over by William Waddell whose family continued to run it until 1977, when it ceased production. It is now used as a retail outlet for woollen goods produced in the Borders, as well as an exhibition centre giving the mill's history.

Hand weaving at Otterburn Mill in 1920. Power loom weaving had been introduced to keep pace with the demand for some of the mill's more famous products such as their rugs. However, some hand looms were retained for specialised production, such as the one shown here. The weaver is passing the shuttle between the warp threads to make the weave.

Plashetts during the First World War. This was the largest colliery in the North Tyne valley. The railway line from the mines can be seen here, before it joins the main track of the Border Counties railway. To the left are the chimney and kilns of the brick factory connected with the mines. In the central background can be seen the powerhouse for the ropeway which hauled the trucks up the incline to Plashetts village and the mines. On the right is the screening plant where the newly-mined coal was sorted and graded prior to being shipped out by rail.

Hawkhope Hill Colliery, Falstone in 1910. This colliery was situated just above the village of Falstone and worked by the Falstone Coal Company. Rights to mine coal were leased by the company at £50 per year from the Ridley family of Park End near Wark. The family also owned the Hawkhope Hill Farm. The pumping engine for the mine can be seen in the centre of the photograph. On the bottom left is one of the entrances to the mine.

Carriteth Moor near Bellingham in the 1920s. The last recorded mine in the Carriteth area was worked from 1910 to 1927 but there is also considerable evidence of other mine works on High Carriteth Farm where the two cottages shown here were situated. The cottages provided accommodation for miners in the area.

Hareshaw Head Colliery in the early twentieth century. This view shows the mine shaft sunk to the north of Bellingham. This mine was flooded during the same thunderstorm which caused a flash flood in Bellingham in May 1911. A number of pit ponies were drowned and some equipment was destroyed. This led to the abandonment of the mine. A series of drift mines were then opened to enable the coal to be mined more safely.

Some Hareshaw pitmen. This group, which was part of a workforce of about thirty men and boys, all worked for Barty Armstrong in the Hareshaw Head drift mines between the two world wars. The first four, from left to right, are: Billy 'Button' Dodd, Billy Elliott (the mine joiner), Jack Hutton who later became pit deputy and James Ridley. The last man on the right is Jock Mason.

Hareshaw Pit houses. These cottages were built north of Bellingham on the Otterburn road for workers in the drift mines. The gardens, in one of which two bee-hives can be seen, were cultivated to produce vegetables for each family. There were five houses in this row. The families which occupied them were, from right to left, the Bells, Huttons, Richardsons, Dodds and Halls.

Elsdon Pit at the time of the First World War. Coal was mined in the Elsdon area from the Middle Ages on. This pit was opened in the 1880s just outside the village near the road to Otterburn. The pit employed up to twenty-five miners and played an important part in the village economy until its closure in the 1960s.

Blaxter Quarry, *c.* 1930. This quarry was opened in the early nineteenth century to provide grey sandstone for building purposes. Such stone was easily quarried and large quantities were produced over the next hundred years. The quarry's commercial capacities were eventually exhausted, leading to closure in 1984. However, it is still occasionally worked when small quantities of stone are required for a special purpose.

Dressed stone blocks at Blaxter, *c.* 1930. Stone from this quarry was used for the construction of buildings in Edinburgh, Glasgow and other cities in Britain where high quality grey sandstone was required. The quarry manager is shown here, about to dispatch a quantity of dressed stone to Knowesgate Station from where it would be conveyed by rail to its destination.

Loading stone blocks at Knowesgate Station, *c.* 1925. This station was opened in 1863 and was the terminus for the Wansbeck Valley railway until the extension of the line to Redesmouth in 1865. Knowesgate was designated the loading point for stone quarried from the Elsdon and later the Blaxter quarries. The County Council also used the station for roadstone deliveries when they opened Whitehill Quarry in the vicinity of Knowesgate. The photograph shows the way in which large stone blocks were loaded on to railway trucks.

Roadmaking near Otterburn, *c.* 1920. Many roads in Redesdale were covered with tarmacadam only after the Second World War. Prior to this, graded stones and gravel had been laid by hand and then compressed by steamroller as shown here. Whinstone, obtained from the Whitehill County Council Quarry, was generally used for this purpose.

The Foundry at Bellingham, c. 1930. Some of the buildings erected by the Hareshaw Iron Works can still be seen in this photograph. On the right are the premises built to house the manager and the officers of the company. The buildings on the left became a brick and tile works after the closure of the Iron Works. The Iron Works was in operation from 1838 to 1848, mining the iron ore and coal found in the hills around Bellingham in order to produce pig iron. The three blast furnaces and other buildings used in this production were originally sited in the foundry yard. This is now the site of Foundry Farm and an industrial estate.

Hareshaw low dam, c. 1920. Situated on the Hareshaw Burn north of Bellingham, the dam was 31 feet wide and 20 feet high. It was erected in the late 1830s to provide water for a water wheel used to power one of the three blast furnaces of the Iron Works. The disused dam survived the 1911 flood but collapsed following a flash flood on 13 September 1968. The remains of the dam can still be seen from the public footpath leading to the waterfall on Hareshaw Burn.

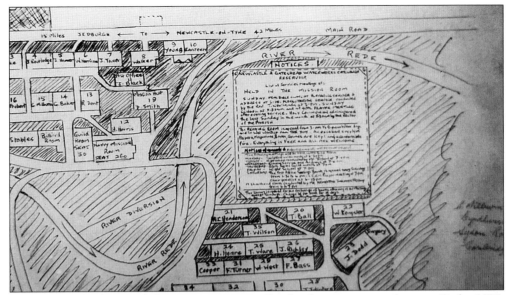

The plan of the huts and the mission room at Catcleugh reservoir on the river Rede, 1899. Catcleugh was constructed by the Whittle Dean Water Company in answer to a steadily increasing demand by the city of Newcastle for additional clean water supplies. When work began in 1894 it became clear that the workers would have to be housed on site. Two villages of huts, called Newcastle and Gateshead, were built on opposite sides of the river by the company for the workforce. By 1899 approximately 504 people were housed in 47 huts at the site.

Catcleugh workmen at the end of the river tunnel completed in 1899. When permission was granted to the Water Company to construct the dam, one of the conditions stipulated that the company had to discharge a certain amount of water into the River Rede both during and after construction. Thus, the tunnel was one of the first parts of the construction to be completed.

Discarded shovels on the Catcleugh site in 1901. A workforce of between 450 and 500 labourers, working with shovels, carried out the initial excavation work on the dam. However, the remoteness of the location and the higher wages offered by railway construction companies meant that it was difficult to keep the Catcleugh workforce up to strength. To overcome the shortage, a steam excavator was purchased and some hand work discontinued, leading to discarded shovels and disgruntled comments.

Automation at Catcleugh in 1901. The machine purchased by the company was a Ruston Steam Excavator, shown in operation here.

At the Waterworks, Catcleugh, *c*. 1900. This postcard, published by a Jedburgh firm, gives an idea of what the hut villages inhabited by the Catcleugh workers looked like at the time. A hut typically consisted of a kitchen, living room, two bedrooms and a wash house. It was large enough to accommodate a family and occasionally a lodger. The large building on the right is the mission room provided by the Water Company for the men and their families to use for church services and social occasions.

Looking up Byewash & Bridge 11/6/04

Looking up the byewash to the bridge in June 1904. The byewash, or spillway, is an important part of any dam structure, as when the reservoir is full it permits excess water to bypass the dam and be discharged into the river. By November of 1905, the entire Catcleugh reservoir project was complete and water was being supplied to Tyneside.

Yarrow Farm and the North Tyne in 1927. This property was owned by the Sisterson family, a female member of which had been born there in 1761 and died there in 1858 at the age of 97. She was reputed to have never been more than six miles from the place of her birth during her long life! The photograph is taken from the Hawkhope Hill area above Falstone. The view from this location is completely different today, as Kielder Forest covers the landscape to the left, while the great bank of the Kielder Dam stands to the right of Yarrow Farm.

Whickhope valley, c. 1920. Nowadays, Whickhope is the name of a long inlet on the south shore of Kielder Water, where the cruiser slipway is located. This photograph shows the Whickhope valley before the Kielder Dam was constructed and the whole area flooded. The building in the foreground was Whickhope Lodge, a shooting box built around 1850 for the fourth Duke of Northumberland who let it to sportsmen for grouse shooting. Whickhope farmhouse can be seen in the background. The farm was over 2,850 acres in size and carried over 1,200 sheep and a herd of twenty cows.

Otterstone Lee in 1914. Located on the south bank of the River Tyne about three miles west of Falstone village, this farm was part of the Mounces estate and belonged to the Swinburne family of Capheaton Hall, one of the oldest families in Northumberland. Otterstone Lee and its subsidiary farms, Longhouse and Mounces Park, covered in excess of 9,100 acres, making it the largest farm in the North Tyne valley. Parts of the farm have now been planted with trees by the Forestry Commission and some of the fields near the river have recently been flooded by the waters of Kielder.

Kielder Dam and Reservoir in 1997. This shows the Kielder Dam from the bank below Hawkhope facing west in the direction of Whickhope and Cranecleugh. Such places shared the fate of many other houses and farms in the North Tyne valley and now lie beneath the calm surface of the reservoir. The hills beyond the dam and lake are all part of the 100,000 acres surrounding Kielder now planted with trees by the Forestry Commission. These developments have completely altered the topography of the valley.

The Fox and Hounds in West Woodburn, between the world wars. When the stone bridge over the River Rede was built around 1800, the amount of travellers passing through the village increased. This hostelry (first known as the Brandy Bank Inn), together with the Bay Horse Inn by the river, answered the need for extra accommodation and was a popular halting place for motorists and cyclists.

The Simpson family outside their shop, c. 1911. Simpson's shop was located just off the main road in West Woodburn. Tommy Simpson is seen on the right next to his wife and other family members. The family lived at Low Park outside the main village but conducted their business in the village.

Tommy Simpson's horse-drawn delivery cart, *c.* 1911. In addition to his shop and some houses, Tommy Simpson also owned a depot further up the valley at Bennetsfield near Otterburn. From the depot and shop, delivery carts carried meal, animal feeds and groceries to the outlying farms and houses in the Rede valley, thus providing an efficient home delivery service.

Right away amongst the Redewater Hills.

—Far from the maddening throng—you will find a Wonderful Store, where almost everything useful for the Home and Farm can be had. Strangers calling are surprised and wonder where the customers come from. Such a stock! Tea for the Housewife; Baccy for the Man; Cigs for the Lads; Chocolates for the Lasses; Boots for all. Drapery and Clothing—the right sort for country wear. Headache, Heartache, and Mange Cures. A Sheepfoot Knife or Likely Wife recommended. Satisfaction guaranteed. No more Ticks, Lice, or Louping Ill. Use the " Border " Dip, sold here. Also all other good makes. Glass, China, Earthenware, Hardware, Mangles, Sewing Machines, Clocks, Watches, Barometers, Oils, Keel Paint, Licensed Dealer in Poisons. Veterinary and Patent Medicines, &c., &c.

—TRY—

Matthew Graham,
Rochester,

Also at Ridsdale and Woodburn Station.

An advertisement for Matthew Graham's three shops, published by the *Reedwetter Review* in 1917. The advertisement was written by Sarah Graham, Matthew's daughter.

The village shop at Otterburn, *c.* 1922. This has now become the village post office as well, but at that time the post office was located on the opposite side of the road. The sign above the door refers to the owner, Margaret Mitchell, who can be seen on the left. Hers was a grocery and drapery store, but it was also a licensed tobacconists and sold refreshments.

A delivery of groceries to Emblehope, *c.* 1930. One of the large sheep farms in the hills of the North Tyne valley, Emblehope was owned by the Duke of Northumberland. The delivery of groceries to outlying farms was never an easy task but Andrew Robinson, who had a shop at Lanehead in Tarset, conveyed small orders to his customers on horseback.

Five

The Army

Hareshaw Common artillery camp at Bellingham, *c.* 1918. Land was first purchased by the Army in the Rede valley for training purposes in 1911. Initially, the land was used for artillery training. The main camping area for soldiers using the ranges was at Birdhopecraig near Rochester but other areas were also used during the First World War. The camp shown here was on Hareshaw Common to the east of Dere Street (the A68), the route used by soldiers when travelling to the ranges from the station at West Woodburn.

ARRIVAL AT WOODBURN STATION.

FOR REDESDALE CAMP.

An arrival at West Woodburn Station bound for Redesdale Camp, during the First World War. This station was well-equipped with cranes, loading docks and sidings, having been used in ferrying stone from the local quarries. It was thus an ideal disembarkation point for the Army *en route* to the Redesdale training area. The station was used by the Army as its main supply point from 1911 to 1947 and on a less frequent basis up to the closure of the line in the 1960s. The arrival of a Field Artillery Unit is shown here; the soldiers are in the carriages in the foreground, the guns are on the open trucks behind them and in the background, to the right, nearest to the engine, are the wagons used to transport the horses.

Trooper Wallace of the Northumberland Yeomanry, *c.* 1880. This was one of the voluntary forces organised to supplement the small British Regular Army between 1852 and the formation of the Territorial Army in 1907. Bill Wallace, a West Woodburn man, poses here, in full uniform and mounted for a parade of his local unit.

A battery of Royal Field Artillery at West Woodburn, *c.* 1914. The men, horses and equipment were disembarked at West Woodburn Station and the horses harnessed up so that they could take the guns to the training grounds at Upper Redesdale.

Gun testing at The Steel in the 1930s. Lord Armstrong operated the foundry and iron mines at Ridsdale from 1864 to 1879. In addition, he tested his guns in the area of Broomhope and The Steel, a practice which continued after the iron works closed. The photograph shows the testing of a gun which was to be fitted on to a British battleship.

An Army tank in Redesdale, c. 1925. During the period between the two world wars, the Army regularly sent tanks to the ranges to test their manoeuvrability and accuracy. The tank shown here is a Vickers Medium Tank Mark II, which was designed in 1922. The Army took delivery of the first of these models in 1924 and used them from then until 1938 as regular weapons and thereafter for training purposes until they were phased out in 1941. The various versions of this tank weighed between sixteen and eighteen tons and were suitable for traversing the ranges. Later tanks were too heavy for the peat soil of Upper Redesdale and tank training ceased here after the Second World War.

Six

Transport

Plashetts railway, *c.* 1900. Miners are being transported back from their work at the mines by a horse-drawn train of coal tubs. Some local youngsters are posing on the tubs as well. In the background the village shop can be seen. The whole village was dependent on the railway deliveries of food and other goods.

Falstone Station in the 1920s. When first built, the station had consisted of a small platform and a single building, with a coal and lime depot at the northern end. In 1895 the station was enlarged to include the station master's house, offices and signal box as shown here. Of the three lines shown, the central line was the through-line between Hexham and Scotland. The station and other buildings are used today as the offices and depot of Forest Enterprise, the successor to the Forestry Commission.

A train in snow near West Woodburn in 1947. The winter of 1947 was one of the worst in living memory, with huge snowfalls and heavy frosts during February and March. In the February blizzards a train on the way from Redesmouth to Morpeth was buried in a snowdrift at Summit Cottages in the Wanney Hills, a couple of miles beyond West Woodburn.

Rescuing the train in 1947. Once weather conditions eased, efforts were made to free the buried train. This view shows the snow plough mounted on an engine, which was used to clear the line. The two men on the left are H. Pigg and W. Scott standing beside a local farmer called William Telfer.

Rescue operations were not straightforward as the train was deeply buried in impacted snow, making it impossible for the snow plough to cope. Snow blowers had not yet been invented so the real work of recovery was undertaken by teams of men hand digging the engines out of the snowdrift. The train was rescued and taken back to Redesmouth Station.

The 'Otterburn', *c.* 1900. Materials had to be transported from West Woodburn Station to Catcleugh during the construction of the dam. A narrow gauge railway line was built between Woodburn and Catcleugh. 'Otterburn' was one of the seven small saddle tank engines which were used on the line. These continued to transport both freight and workers until the completion of the dam in 1905.

Rebuilding West Woodburn Bridge in 1957. The first bridge over the Rede at West Woodburn was constructed at the end of the eighteenth century. Increased traffic over the bridge weakened its structure and it was reconstructed in the 1950s. Workmen are seen here at work strengthening the bridge's foundations.

Mail dispatch at Otterburn, *c.* 1920. The building now occupied by Lloyd's Bank in Otterburn was used as the village post office in the 1920s and early '30s. The Bellingham doctor also held his weekly surgeries here every Tuesday. The sub-postmaster, Mr Stanley Potts, is in the centre of the photograph, surrounded by the local postmen and their various modes of transport for delivering parcels and letters to the outlying villages and farms.

Captain Dawes' bi-plane at Otterburn Hall, October 1913. When Lord James Murray's daughter sold Otterburn Hall, it was purchased by Sir Charles and Lady Morrison-Bell. In October 1913 Lady Morrison-Bell was visited by her nephew, Captain G.W. Dawes of the Royal Flying Corps, during his flight from York to Montrose. Before Captain Dawes resumed his flight, the Maurice Farnham bi-plane was proudly displayed to the local people. This was also the first recorded landing and take-off by an aircraft in the Rede valley.

Transport horses from the North Tyne valley, in Bellingham in 1915. Taken in front of the Town Hall, this is a poignant reminder of the sacrifices made by ordinary people during the First World War. From the beginning of the war the British Army needed vast quantities of riding and draught horses. Requisition officers were appointed and given the directive to collect in excess of a hundred thousand horses of all types for the war effort. By the end of September 1914, nine thousand working horses from farms in southern England had been collected and sent overseas, never to return. As the war progressed horses continued to be requisitioned throughout the country by the Army. This photograph shows the sad assembly of farm horses from around Bellingham and the valleys. The requisitioning officer can be seen under the clock tower of the Town Hall, surrounded by the animals and their owners, who were bidding farewell not only to the key workers on their farms but also to devoted, much loved companions.

Seven
Education and Worship

Lord Redesdale's School at Rochester in 1896. Lord Redesdale had the school built in 1850 and endowed it with a sum of £10 per annum. A house and garden attached provided living accommodation for the teacher. The average attendance at the time of this photograph was thirty-eight although the schoolroom could take sixty children. The schoolchildren and master, Ralph Goundry, are shown here in front of the school porch. The school was closed in 1953 and the pupils transferred to Otterburn School.

Corsenside Parish School in 1919. This school was opened at West Woodburn in 1818 on land given by the Revd Anthony Hunter. It had accommodation for 125 children initially but was enlarged in 1883 to take up to 215 children. At least two teachers taught in the school. The photograph shows the younger of the two classes of 1919, taught by the wife of the headmaster, Mrs Alvey, who stands on the right.

Brown Rigg Camp School, Bellingham in the 1950s. This school was opened by the National Camps Corporation, a body dedicated to promoting healthier open air schooling for children. Used during the war years as a refuge for evacuees from Tyneside and elsewhere, it afterwards became a residential senior school offering courses to pupils drawn from all parts of the county. The school was modified to provide regular residential secondary education for 175 pupils in the 1960s. Declining numbers and financial difficulties caused its closure in 1985 and the site and buildings have now been turned into a holiday centre and caravan site.

Thorneyburn church in 1920. The parish of Thorneyburn was formed after the break up of the massive Simonburn parish into a number of smaller parishes by the commissioners of the Greenwich Hospital estates in 1811. Dedicated to St Aidan, it was built to the design of the architect H.H. Seward, who also designed the churches at Greystead, Humshaugh and Wark. It was intended that the church, which is used by the village of Greenhaugh, would be served by retired naval chaplains. The church no longer has its own minister and services are carried out by the vicars of Bellingham and Falstone.

The re-opening of the West Woodburn Methodist chapel in 1906. The United Free Methodist church raised the sum of £220 to purchase land in 1866 and erected a chapel on the edge of what is now the green area in front of Whiteacre. By the early twentieth century the building was in poor repair and the photograph shows the congregation at the grand re-opening in 1906 after repairs had been completed. The building seated 180 although the congregation was never that large.

The rectory at Bellingham, *c.* 1920. In 1818 the church commissioners engaged the architect H.H. Seward to build a rectory, complete with coach house and outbuildings, for St Cuthbert's church using the same design as for Wark, Thorneyburn and other North Tyne churches. The house was used by the vicar until the 1990s when it was sold and a modern vicarage built beside it.

The Presbyterian church and manse at Bellingham, *c.* 1920. Prior to the legalisation of their faith in the late eighteenth century, Presbyterians were often forced to meet secretly for worship in remote places such as Padon Hill. The first official Presbyterian church in Bellingham was opened in 1803, but was replaced in 1883 by the church shown above, which could seat up to 300 people. The manse was completed a few months after the church. Both buildings are now privately owned. This photograph was taken before the construction of the council houses in Fairshaw Crescent.

Eight

Sport and Leisure

Ridsdale tennis club, *c.* 1925. Sports teams flourished in all the villages of the Rede and North Tyne in the 1920s and '30s. This tennis club was quite a formidable force in the Rede valley. Those who have been identified in this photograph are Howard Graham, seated front left, the sisters Nan and Isabella Walton in the second row and Sarah Graham on the extreme right.

Ridsdale cricket club, *c.* 1910. This was another local team, complete with scorer and twelfth man!

West Woodburn cricket team in 1907. Only the required eleven men are present on this occasion but note the two umpires! Septimus Charlton, who appears in both pictures on this page, is the figure on the right in the front holding a cricket bat.

West Woodburn AFC in 1947-48. The team is pictured with the famous Chipchase Cup for which there was strong competition among the local village teams. Ronnie Charlton, the son of Septimus Charlton (see opposite page), who was responsible for collecting many of the Redesdale Society photographs used in this book, is kneeling second from left.

West Woodburn brass band, c. 1910. The band had been invited over to Bellingham by one of the local publicans and is shown here outside the Rose and Crown in Manchester Square, a building which looks quite different today. The band was taken around the village on the horse-drawn cart and had probably been engaged to play during the local custom of riding the fair.

Riding the fair at Bellingham in 1904. St Cuthbert's fair was held on the first Saturday after 16 September. This was one of the largest wool fairs in the county when farmers from all over Tynedale and Redesdale sold their wool clips to buyers from the wool towns of the Borders. One of the notable features of this fair was the custom of 'the riding of the fair', when a group of local people rode around the boundaries of the town to ensure that they had not been encroached upon by strangers. At the end of the ride the town charter was ceremoniously read aloud. The Duke of Northumberland's man, Mr Gardiner, carries the town flag, while the riders gather outside the Rose and Crown. The Northumbrian piper prepares to pipe them on their ride. The tradition is very similar to the common ridings held in Scottish towns just over the border.

A shooting party on the Wanney Hills, *c.* 1914. Shooting was a popular local sport and this group is shown on part of the Ray estate, which was owned by the engineer Sir Charles Parsons. A moderate bag of game is stretched out in front of the men. Note that no hares have been shot as they were reserved for the sport of hare coursing, also very popular in the North Tyne and Rede valleys before the First World War.

Bellingham golf course, *c.* 1920. The golf club moved from the Fairstead to become tenants of Boggle Hole Farm, owned by the Duke of Northumberland in 1906. The pavilion or club house can be seen in the centre rear on the top of the hill as the farmstead was used for agricultural purposes at that time and did not become the present club house until 1972. The fourth green can be seen in the foreground. Sheep were permitted to graze the course at that time but fences ensured that they did not trespass on the greens. The club finally bought out the grazing rights in the 1970s.

North Tyne Foxhounds meet at Redeswood, Bellingham in 1915. Fox hunting was one of the leading country field sports during the nineteenth century. In the North Tyne and Rede valleys the hunts were usually run by farmers as an important method of controlling foxes which were an ever-present danger to the large sheep flocks in these areas. The meet shown here took place at Redeswood Farm, a property owned by the Charlton family of Hesleyside. The group is enjoying a stirrup cup before setting out. The pack, never more than eight couples, was under the control of Mr Murray of the Smale Farm, higher up in the valley. He had taken over as Master of Hounds in 1910, on the death of Tom Robson. The varied garb of the riders is probably the result of wartime privations.

Nine
Historical Landmarks and Occasions

Castles, Memorials and Jubilees and other events

Blessing the War Memorial at West Woodburn in 1921. After the First World War, memorials were erected all over Great Britain in remembrance of those who had died and those who had served and survived. The villagers of East and West Woodburn and Ridsdale raised money by subscription to erect their memorial on land near the station. The grey granite obelisk was purchased for £300 and erected, although only enough money remained to record the names of the sixteen men who had died in the War.

The site of Dally Castle, Tarset, c. 1920. In the thirteenth century Tynedale was controlled by Alexander II, king of the Scots, who gave his sister Margaret the area of Chirdon in the North Tyne valley in 1221. She gave Chirdon to the Scottish nobleman Sir David Lindsay who built Dally Castle. In the nineteenth century the ruined castle, on the site of which a farm and water mill had been built, passed into the ownership of the Haggerston family. The mill can be seen nearest to the stream while the remains of the castle can be discerned to the left of the farmhouse at the rear.

Sidwood, c. 1940. This was the estate of the Watson family in the valley of the Tarset Burn, north-west of Greenhaugh. The property extended to almost 2,000 acres and included farms such as Gleedlee, Newbiggin and Redheugh. When the family was not in residence, the house was leased out, together with the shooting rights. The last member of the Watson family sold the house and estate in 1926. The house subsequently fell into disrepair and was demolished some years ago. The Forestry Commission purchased the site of the house and part of the estate and planted it with trees.

West Woodburn Jubilee March, 1935. This parade was one of the events staged in the valleys to celebrate the Silver Jubilee of King George V's Coronation. In Woodburn, villagers paraded down the main street on the way to the village picnic. Houses were decorated with bunting for the event.

Mounces Hall near Kielder in 1929. Built by Sir John Swinburne around 1833, it was used by the family for holidays and as a base for management of their estate in North Tynedale. Later it was let as a shooting lodge with rights on the estate. This photograph shows the hall three years before the Swinburnes sold the estate. By this time the hall boasted two living-rooms, nine principal bedrooms, substantial servants' quarters and an indoor lavatory. The ruins of the hall now lie beneath the waters of Kielder Reservoir.

Troughend Hall near Otterburn, c. 1910. The hall was the home of the Reeds, one of the oldest families in Redesdale. Built by Elrington Reed, a prominent member of the family who died in 1758, it replaced the fortified tower which was the family's former home. This branch of the Reed family sold the estate to the Reeds of Chipchase in the eighteenth century. Thereafter, it passed through numerous owners, one of whom demolished the hall a number of years ago.

Haughton ferry at Humshaugh in 1907. The fact that there is no bridge over the North Tyne river between Chollerford and Wark is not a serious problem in this age of motorised transport. However, it was a serious difficulty in the past and a hand-operated ferry was established at Haughton in order to provide a service between the villages of Humshaugh and Barrasford. The ferryman lived in the house on the west bank of the river and could be summoned to the east bank by ringing a bell. The ferry is believed to have continued to operate until 1958.

Peace celebrations at West Woodburn. Communal peace celebrations were held all over the country in 1919. Here we see the children's picnic held in the garden of one of the larger houses at West Woodburn. The headmaster, Mr Alvey and his wife can be seen in the background, no doubt having played a major part in the organisation of this event.

This photograph was taken outside Graham's stores, Sarelaw Cottages, Ridsdale, in 1910 on the occasion of the marriage of Richard Brown and Ellen Graham. The bride's mother is seated next to the groom, whilst her father, Matthew Graham, sits next to her holding her brother Howard on his knee. Sarah Graham is standing on the extreme left.

The Earl of Redesdale, *c.* 1880. This shows John Thomas Freeman-Mitford, the second Lord Redesdale, who was born in 1805 and succeeded to the title in 1830. Educated at Eton and Oxford, Lord Redesdale was politically active throughout his lifetime. He was made Chairman of Committees and Deputy Speaker of the House of Lords in 1851, an office he held until his death in 1886. In recognition of his important work in helping to frame and bring into law the Appelate Jurisdiction Act, he was created the Earl of Redesdale in 1877. His was the largest estate in the Rede valley at over 17,000 acres. On his death the estate, but not the title, passed to his cousin A.B. Freeman-Mitford, who was created Lord Redesdale in 1902.

Acknowledgements

The photographs used in this book have been taken from four main sources: the collection of glass photographic slides taken by Ted Dobbin of Bellingham, now in the possession of Frank Mattinson and loaned for copying to the Northumberland Library; the collection of photographic material assembled by the late Viktor Blankenburgs and now held in the Northumberland Record Office; the collection of photographs, postcards and personal memorabilia about Wark owned by Cyril Cooper; lastly, the Redesdale Society's collection of photographic slides of postcards, photographs and pictures of the Rede valley and neighbouring areas. We owe grateful thanks to the owners and custodians of all this material for their kindness in allowing us to use it in this book.

We are also indebted to the following: Ben Anderson, John Bacon, Dorothy and Jim Bell, the Bellingham Heritage Centre, Muriel and Tommy Breckons, Jim Brownbridge, Pat Cameron, Jim Charlton, the late Ronnie Charlton, Kath Chruszczewski, Cyril Cooper, the late Aynesly Glass, Frank Mattinson, Jim Mulholland, Diana Murray, Ian Mungall, John and Vicky Roberts, Sadie Robson, Glenys and Michael Telfer, Johnnie Telfer and Ettie Young for generously providing us with information. For revisions to some captions we are grateful to Bill Dickinson, Stan Owen, Tommy Simpson and Muriel Ward.

We received support, technical assistance and encouragement from the following and are deeply grateful: Sally Bird, Head of Heritage for Northumberland County Council and Jonathan West of Newcastle University. Our thanks to Mark Benjamin for suggesting the original project and to Andrew Clark of Chalford Publishing for his advice.

The authors would be delighted to hear from anyone who may have further information about photographs used in this book.